PRIMARY SCRIPTURES

Book of Mormon Stories for Kids

Volume 3 • 3 Nephi–Moroni

Text adapted by Jason Zippro　　Illustrated by Alycia Pace

This book belongs to:

_____

PRIMARY SCRIPTURES

Book of Mormon Stories for Kids

Volume 3 • 3 Nephi–Moroni

Text adapted by Jason Zippro
Illustrated by Alycia Pace

© Primary Scriptures, LLC
All Rights Reserved.

No part of this book may be reproduced in any form whatsoever, whether by graphic, visual, electronic, film, microfilm, tape recording, or any other means, without the written consent of the author, except in the case of brief passages embodied in critical reviews or articles.

This is not an official publication of the Church of Jesus Christ of Latter-day Saints. The opinions and views expressed herein belong solely to the author and do not necessarily represent the opinions and views of the Church.

ISBN 13: 978-1-7349053-1-1

REL046000 RELIGION / Christianity / Church of Jesus Christ of Latter-day Saints (Mormon)
REL091000 RELIGION / Christian Education / Children & Youth
JNF049200 JUVENILE NONFICTION / Religious / Christian / Early Readers

Cover design © 2020 Primary Scriptures, LLC
Illustrations by Alycia Pace
Cover design by Angela Baxter
Edited and typeset by Emily Chambers

10 9 8 7 6 5 4 3 2 1

www.PrimaryScriptures.com

Contents

3RD & 4TH NEPHI   1

The Sign of Jesus Christ's Birth   3
3 NEPHI 1

Lachoneus Defends against the Robbers   10
3 NEPHI 2–3

The Nephites Defeat the Robbers   20
3 NEPHI 4

The Nephites Repent and Preach   28
3 NEPHI 5

Mormon Writes the History of the Nephites   31
3 NEPHI 5

The Nephites Grow Rich and Wicked   35
3 NEPHI 6

The Nephites Break Apart into Tribes   42
3 NEPHI 7

The Signs of Jesus Christ's Death   48
3 NEPHI 8

Jesus Christ Speaks to the Nephites from Heaven   54
3 NEPHI 9

Prophets Always Warn the People before Destruction 3 NEPHI 10	58
Jesus Christ Descends from Heaven 3 NEPHI 11	62
Jesus Christ Teaches How To Baptize 3 NEPHI 11–12	69
Jesus Christ Speaks the Beatitudes 3 NEPHI 12	74
Jesus Christ Commands Us To Obey a Higher Law 3 NEPHI 12	78
Jesus Christ Teaches about Prayer and Prophets 3 NEPHI 13–14	85
Jesus Christ Has Many Sheep 3 NEPHI 15–16	92
Jesus Christ Heals the People and Blesses the Children 3 NEPHI 17	95
Jesus Christ Teaches about the Sacrament 3 NEPHI 18	101
The Nephite Disciples Teach and Are Baptized 3 NEPHI 19	108

Jesus Christ Prophesies of the Last Days   115
3 NEPHI 20–23, 29–30

The Prophet Malachi's Words   123
3 NEPHI 24–25

The Disciples Continue To Teach and Baptize   130
3 NEPHI 26

Jesus Christ Appears Again
to the Nephite Disciples   134
3 NEPHI 27–28

Three Hundred Years of Nephite Righteousness   146
4 NEPHI

MORMON   155

Mormon Is Visited by Jesus Christ   157
MORMON 1

Mormon Commands the Nephite Army   160
MORMON 2

Mormon Preaches to the Nephites   166
MORMON 3

Mormon Gathers the Nephite Records   171
MORMON 4

The Book of Mormon Testifies of Jesus Christ   174
MORMON 5

The Battle at Cumorah MORMON 6	178
Mormon's Testimony MORMON 7	181
Moroni Gets the Plates MORMON 8	184
Moroni Writes to Us in the Latter Days MORMON 9	188

ETHER 193

God Doesn't Change the Jaredite Language ETHER 1	195
The Jaredites Travel and Build Boats ETHER 2	200
Mahonri Sees Jesus Christ ETHER 3	211
Moroni Adds the Jaredite Records to the Gold Plates ETHER 4–5	219
The Jaredites Multiply and Choose a King ETHER 6	224
The Jaredites Begin To Fight Each Other ETHER 7	232

Akish and the Secret Society   246
ETHER 8

The Jaredites Nearly Destroy Themselves   252
ETHER 9

Wicked Kings Lead to Destruction   261
ETHER 10–11

Faith, Hope, and Grace   267
ETHER 12

The Prophet Ether Warns King Coriantumr   281
ETHER 13

Coriantumr Fights Gilead, Lib, Then Shiz   288
ETHER 14

The Jaredites Completely Destroy Themselves   293
ETHER 15

MORONI   301

Laying on of Hands, Ordaining,
and the Sacrament   303
MORONI 1–5

Being Members of The Church of Jesus Christ   307
MORONI 6

Mormon Teaches about
Faith, Hope, and Charity   312
MORONI 7

Mormon Teaches about Baptism MORONI 8	320
The Nephites and Lamanites Are Wicked MORONI 9	324
Moroni's Final Testimony MORONI 10	329
ABOUT THE AUTHOR & ILLUSTRATOR	334

3rd & 4th Nephi

The Sign of Jesus Christ's Birth
3 NEPHI 1

Nephi the prophet gave all the Nephite records to his son. Nephi traveled out of the land and was never seen or heard from again.

Nephi's son was also named Nephi. He began to write down what happened to the people in his day. He wrote that many of the signs and miracles the prophets spoke about began to come true.

Many Nephites didn't believe the prophecies. They said Samuel's sign would've happened by now if it were true. The unbelievers decided to kill all the believers if the sign didn't happen by a certain day.

3 NEPHI 1

The believers began to worry the sign wouldn't happen in time. But they trusted Samuel's prophecy and watched for the sign. They waited for the night that would be as bright as day.

3 NEPHI 1

When Nephi learned what the unbelievers planned to do, he prayed to God for help. Jesus spoke to him, "Nephi, be calm and don't worry. Tomorrow I will be born. So tonight the sign will be given."

3 NEPHI 1

That night the sun went down, but the night sky didn't get dark. Everyone was amazed. Many unbelievers fell to the ground because they were so shocked. What Samuel the prophet had said did come true!

3 NEPHI 1

As prophesied, a new star appeared in the sky. In the morning, the sun came up like it normally did. Many unbelievers began to believe and repent of their sins. So, Nephi baptized them. And there was peace again.

Lachoneus Defends against the Robbers
3 NEPHI 2–3

Satan began to trick the people. He made the people think the signs didn't happen. He made them think the signs were made-up stories. Many people began to not believe in the signs anymore.

3 NEPHI 2–3

The people began to be very wicked again. They ignored the teachings of the prophets. Many of the Nephites and Lamanites began to join the robbers who lived in the mountains.

The robbers continued to cause trouble. The Nephites and Lamanites gathered together to protect themselves. Thirteen years after Samuel's sign of Christ's birth, a war began against the robbers.

3 NEPHI 2–3

The ruler of the robbers was a man named Giddianhi. He was a wicked man. The ruler of the Nephites and Lamanites was a man named Lachoneus. He was a good man who believed in God.

Giddianhi sent Lachoneus a letter. Giddianhi told Lachoneus they should give up and join the robbers. Giddianhi would command his people to kill all the Nephites and Lamanites if they didn't.

3 NEPHI 2–3

Lachoneus was not afraid. He told his people to repent and pray to God for strength. God would not let the robbers destroy them if they prayed and repented. All the people obeyed Lachoneus.

3 NEPHI 2–3

Lachoneus commanded his people to gather between the cities Zarahemla and Bountiful. Thousands of people came with their families and animals.

3 NEPHI 2–3

Lachoneus had the people prepare for war. He commanded the people to build walls all around to protect them. He sent guards to watch for the robbers day and night. They made weapons, armor, and shields.

3 NEPHI 2–3

Lachoneus organized the Nephite and Lamanite armies. He chose people with the spirit of prophecy to be captains over the armies. The Chief Captain over the entire army was Gidgiddoni.

3 NEPHI 2–3

Gidgiddoni was a great prophet. The people asked him to attack the robbers first. Gidgiddoni refused. He said if they waited for the robbers to attack first, God would help the Nephites and Lamanites to win.

The Nephites Defeat the Robbers
3 NEPHI 4

A few months later, the robbers came to battle the Nephites. The robbers thought the Nephites were afraid because they were kneeling. But the Nephites were praying to God for strength.

3 NEPHI 4

The robbers and Nephites battled very hard. It was the worst battle the Nephites ever had. When the robbers began to lose, they ran away. Gidgiddoni commanded his army to chase the robbers.

3 NEPHI 4

Giddianhi, the leader of the robbers, tried to run away too. He was tired from the battle. The Nephites caught up to him and killed him. The robbers didn't come back for almost two years.

3 NEPHI 4

When the robbers returned, they surrounded the city. They wanted to trap the Nephites inside. They hoped the Nephites would run out of food. But the Nephites had enough food storage for seven years.

23

3 NEPHI 4

The robbers did not have food storage. They could only hunt wild animals. The robbers soon ran out of food and began to starve. Their new leader, Zemnarihah, decided to give up and leave.

Gidgiddoni made a plan to defeat the robbers as they were leaving. He knew the robbers were weak because they were hungry. So Gidgiddoni snuck half his army out of the city at night and waited.

3 NEPHI 4

When the robbers began to leave, Gidgiddoni's army chased the robbers. The robbers tried to run away, but the army hiding outside of the city blocked them. The Nephites surrounded and trapped the robbers.

3 NEPHI 4

Zemnarihah and many robbers were destroyed. But some robbers gave up and became prisoners. The Nephites thanked God. They knew God had protected them from the robbers because they had repented.

The Nephites Repent and Preach
3 NEPHI 5

All of the Nephites believed the prophets. They saw many signs. They knew the signs meant Christ had been born on the earth. Everyone repented of their sins. They eagerly served God day and night.

3 NEPHI 5

The Nephites sent missionaries to teach the robbers in prison. Some robbers promised to never kill again. The Nephites let those robbers go free.

3 NEPHI 5

Many wonderful things happened to the people over the next several years. There were so many good things that happened to them that Nephi couldn't write them all down.

Mormon Writes the History of the Nephites
3 NEPHI 5

Years later, the prophet Mormon took the records of the Nephites. Mormon wrote down many Nephite stories in the Gold Plates.

3 NEPHI 5

Mormon wrote, "I am a follower of Jesus Christ. He asked me to share His words. He wants all of us to live with God. That is why I wrote this record. It tells what happened to the Nephites and Lamanites.

3 NEPHI 5

Heavenly Father and Jesus Christ have given us so much knowledge. They have taught my people how to be saved and live with Them again. Whenever my people obeyed God, He has blessed them.

33

3 NEPHI 5

Someday God will gather His children again from all over the world. He will help them learn the promises He has made with them. And all His children will know their Redeemer, Jesus Christ."

The Nephites Grow Rich and Wicked
3 NEPHI 6

The Nephites began to spread out over the land. They used their food storage to help start their lives again. The Nephites rebuilt many of their cities.

3 NEPHI 6

The Nephites gave any robbers who repented a place to live. Lachoneus, Gidgiddoni, and the other great leaders made new laws. The laws were equal and fair to everyone. The new laws kept peace and order.

3 NEPHI 6

Some Nephites began to make more money than others. Satan made the rich Nephites think that they were better because they were richer.

37

3 NEPHI 6

Over nine years the people became very wicked, even the members of the church. Everyone knew God's commandments, but they chose to disobey them. They cared more about being rich and powerful.

3 NEPHI 6

God began to send prophets to the Nephites. They taught about Jesus Christ. They told the people to repent. Many people became angry with the prophets, but the judges and lawyers were the most angry.

3 NEPHI 6

Secretly, some judges killed a few prophets. When the Chief Governor found out, he brought the judges to Zarahemla. They needed to be punished for killing the prophets.

Many of the other lawyers and judges wanted to protect the judges who killed the prophets. They made a secret society. They decided to kill the Chief Governor and make one of them the king.

The Nephites Break Apart into Tribes
3 NEPHI 7

The leader of the secret society was a man named Jacob. The secret society killed the Chief Governor, hoping to make Jacob king instead. But when the Chief Governor died, the people split into many tribes.

3 NEPHI 7

Each tribe chose their own chief to lead them. All the tribes agreed to not fight each other. But all the tribes hated Jacob's tribe because they had killed the Chief Governor. So Jacob's tribe ran away to safety.

3 NEPHI 7

Even though the people agreed to not fight each other, they were still wicked. They threw stones at the prophets and kicked them out of their cities. So Nephi began to preach to the people too.

3 NEPHI 7

Nephi told the people to repent. He was filled with the Spirit. Angels came down from heaven and visited him every day. He preached the gospel. Anyone who heard him knew what he was saying was true.

3 NEPHI 7

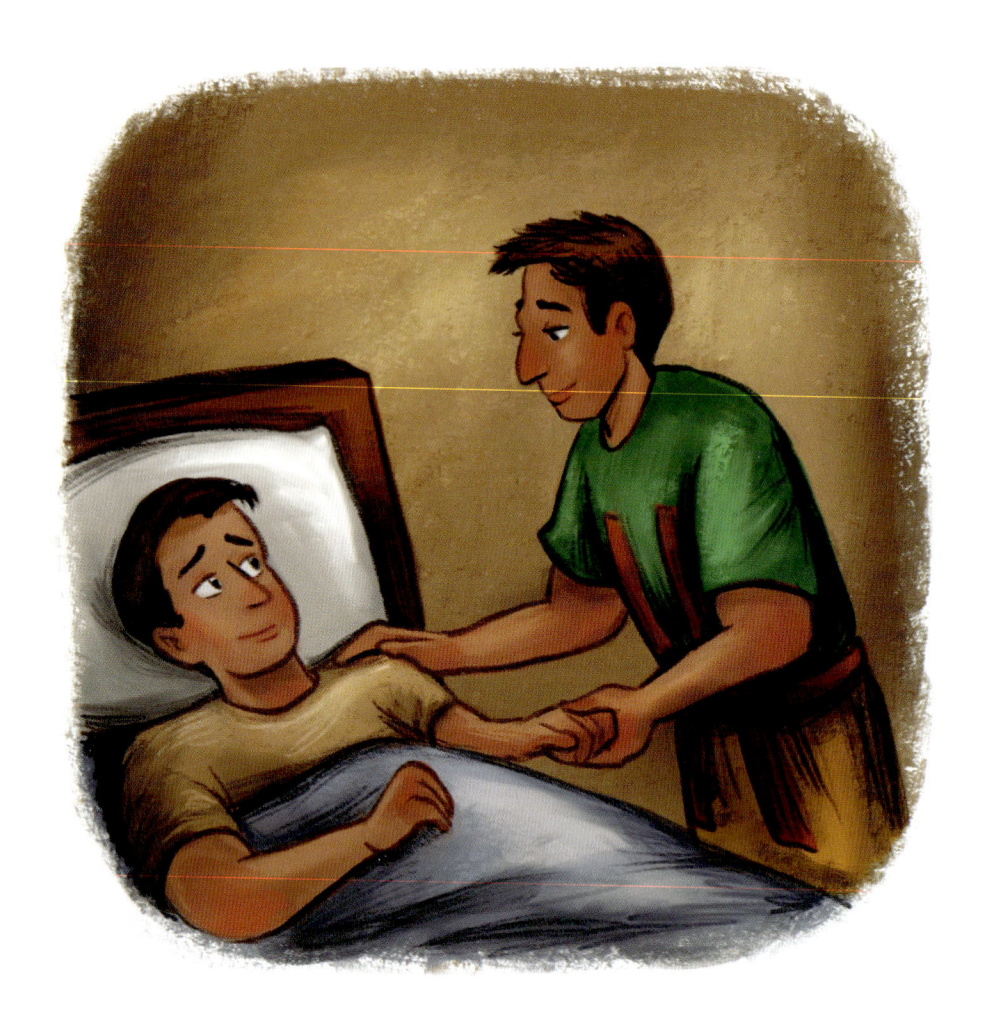

Even though people knew what Nephi said was true, they still didn't change. Many were angry with Nephi because he was so powerful. He cast out evil spirits and even raised his brother from the dead.

Nephi continued to teach the people for more than a year. Very few people repented of their sins. Those who did repent were baptized. But most of the Nephites stayed wicked.

The Signs of Jesus Christ's Death
3 NEPHI 8

Thirty-three years passed since Samuel's sign of a day and a night and a day without any darkness. The people began to look for Samuel's other sign where there would be three days of darkness.

3 NEPHI 8

In the first month of the thirty-fourth year, there was the greatest storm the Nephites had ever seen. There was thunder and lightning. Many cities caught fire. Even the great city of Zarahemla burned.

There were tornadoes, and it poured rain. Every single city was damaged or destroyed. And many cities sank into the sea, like the city of Moroni.

3 NEPHI 8

Earthquakes shook the cities. The roads between the cities broke apart. Rocks cracked, and the ground split open. Several cities were buried, like the city of Moronihah.

51

3 NEPHI 8

All these terrible things happened over three hours. Many people died. When the storms finished, a thick, dark fog covered the land. It blocked out the sun. No one could even light a fire to see.

The darkness lasted three days, just as Samuel had prophesied. During that time, the earth continued to shake. The people wished they had repented sooner. They were sad for those who died in the storms.

Jesus Christ Speaks to the Nephites from Heaven
3 NEPHI 9

On the third day, the people heard a voice. "Beware, my people! Many of my sons and daughters have died because they did not repent. They did not listen to the prophets, but killed them instead.

3 NEPHI 9

I burned many cities and the people in them. I sank many cities into the sea and the people in them. And I buried many cities and the people in them. I did this because they were wicked and did not repent.

3 NEPHI 9

I saved all of you. You were more righteous than those who died. Will you now come to me and repent, so I can heal you? If you come to me, I will show you kindness and love. I will give you eternal life.

3 NEPHI 9

I am Jesus Christ, the Son of God. I created the heavens and the earth. I am the Light and Life of the World. Believe in me. Show me you're sorry for your sins. Repent and I will give you the Holy Ghost. I died and came back to life so you can live with God again. So repent and be saved."

57

Prophets Always Warn the People before Destruction
3 NEPHI 10

All the people were amazed! They stopped crying and were silent. They listened to the voice again, "Oh my people! I tried to gather you like a hen gathers her baby chicks, but you would not come."

3 NEPHI 10

Then the earth stopped shaking. The cracks in the ground shut again. The darkness went away. The people began to thank Jesus Christ. They began to be joyful again.

3 NEPHI 10

Moroni explained that the prophets had warned about the fires, storms, earthquakes, and signs of darkness. But many of the people did not believe and had killed the prophets for warning them.

3 NEPHI 10

Moroni warned, "If you have the scriptures, study them. Read and try to understand them. The prophets write scriptures. The things they write down are to help us be good, and warn us about what will happen."

Jesus Christ Descends from Heaven
3 NEPHI 11

In the city of Bountiful, many people gathered near the temple. They were talking about Jesus Christ. While they were speaking they heard a voice. They did not understand what the voice said.

3 NEPHI 11

The voice was soft and gentle, but it caused their hearts to burn. The people heard the voice a second time. They still did not understand. They looked up at the sky where the voice came from.

3 NEPHI 11

The third time they heard the voice, they listened and understood. The voice said, "Look! This is my beloved Son. I am pleased with Him. He has honored my name. Listen to Him!"

3 NEPHI 11

The people silently watched as a man came down out of heaven. He said, "I am Jesus Christ. The prophets testified I would come. I am the Light of the World. I have taken everyone's sins upon me."

3 NEPHI 11

He said, "Stand and come to me. Feel the marks in my hands, feet, and side. Then you will know I am the Savior of the world. I died to save you all from sin."

3 NEPHI 11

The people went one by one to feel the marks on Jesus's body. When every person finished, they all shouted, "Hosanna! Blessed be the name of the Most High God!" And they all bowed at Jesus Christ's feet.

67

3 NEPHI 11

Then Jesus said, "Nephi, come to me." Nephi came, bowed down, and kissed Jesus's feet. Then Jesus called others to Him. He gave twelve of them the power to baptize.

Jesus Christ Teaches How To Baptize
3 NEPHI 11–12

Jesus Christ taught the twelve how someone should be baptized. "If someone repents of their sins and wants to be baptized, then you can baptize them.

3 NEPHI 11–12

Stand in some water. Then say, 'Having authority given me of Jesus Christ, I baptize you in the name of the Father, and of the Son, and of the Holy Ghost. Amen.'

3 NEPHI 11–12

Then lower them underneath the water until their whole body is covered. Then help them up out of the water. This is how you should baptize.

3 NEPHI 11–12

Repent of your sins. Be baptized in the way I just showed you. Then continue to believe and trust me like small children do. If you do these things, then you will be saved. You will live in heaven again someday."

3 NEPHI 11–12

Then Jesus told the people, "I have chosen these twelve. You will be blessed if you listen and obey them. I have given them power to baptize you. Then you will receive the Holy Ghost, and your sins will be forgiven."

Jesus Christ Speaks the Beatitudes
3 NEPHI 12

Jesus blessed the people saying, "Those who are humble will be blessed to live in God's kingdom. Those who are sad and suffering will be blessed with comfort.

3 NEPHI 12

Those who are gentle and patient will be blessed to enjoy all good things. Those who try to do right things will be blessed with the Holy Ghost. Those who are kind and forgiving will be blessed with forgiveness.

3 NEPHI 12

Those whose hearts are focused on God will be blessed to someday see God. Those who help others be calm and kind will be called the children of God.

3 NEPHI 12

Those who are hurt by others because they chose to follow me, will be blessed to live happily in God's kingdom. Remember that even the prophets before you were hurt for following me."

Jesus Christ Commands Us To Obey a Higher Law
3 NEPHI 12

Jesus taught the people to be good examples to the world. "You are like salt. When you add salt to food, it makes it taste better. You are also like a city on a mountain top—it can be seen from everywhere.

3 NEPHI 12

If you light a candle, do you hide it? No, you use it to shine light so you can see. When you do good things, you are like a light for other people.

3 NEPHI 12

You've been commanded to not kill. But I say, don't even get angry with others. Find a way to help everyone be happy and agree. Try to do this even with people you don't like.

3 NEPHI 12

When you get married, be loyal to your spouse. Be loyal not only in everything you do, but also in everything you think.

81

3 NEPHI 12

If someone asks you to do something, say, 'Yes, I will do that' or 'No, I can't do that.' If you say you're going to do something, do it.

3 NEPHI 12

Care about and forgive others. Love everyone—even your enemies. If they try to do or say mean things to you, pray for them. Don't try to get even. Always be kind in return.

3 NEPHI 12

If you really seek to do good, as if you are hungry for it, then you will be filled with the Holy Ghost. I want you to be perfect like me and Heavenly Father. I have taught you these things to help you be perfect too."

Jesus Christ Teaches about Prayer and Prophets
3 NEPHI 13–14

Jesus taught the people to pray: "'Our Father in heaven, holy is Your name. May Your purposes be done on earth as they are in heaven. Forgive us, as we forgive others.

3 NEPHI 13–14

Help us not want to do bad things. Save us from evil. It is Your kingdom, power, and greatness that will last forever. Amen.'

3 NEPHI 13–14

Choose things that will give you blessings in heaven. Don't focus on things that will only make you rich on earth. Choosing spiritual things will fill you with light. What you focus on is what you care about most.

3 NEPHI 13–14

Ask for what you need, and God will give it to you. Look for what is good, and God will help you find it. Knock on God's door to enter, and He will open it and let you in.

3 NEPHI 13–14

Remember that the path to evil is large and wide. It is easy to follow. There will be many people that follow it. The path to heaven is narrow. There will be very few that follow it.

3 NEPHI 13–14

Follow true prophets. You will know if they are true by what they do. They are like fruit trees. If the tree is a bad tree, the fruit will be bad. But only a good fruit tree can make good fruit.

3 NEPHI 13–14

If you do what I say, you are like a wise man who builds his house on a rock. When it rains, his house will not fall. But a foolish man builds his house on sand. When it rains, his house will wash away."

Jesus Christ Has Many Sheep
3 NEPHI 15–16

Jesus continued to teach the people, "Do not be surprised when I say the old way is done. Now there is a new way. I am the one who gave you the old way, called the Law of Moses. That law is now finished.

3 NEPHI 15–16

I told the people in Jerusalem that I am the shepherd. I told them that I have other sheep that are not in Jerusalem. You are some of the sheep that I was talking about. And there are still other sheep I must visit.

3 NEPHI 15–16

The new way is called the gospel. In the last days, I will bring my gospel to all my sheep. My sheep are called the House of Israel. Everyone else is called a Gentile. I will also bring my gospel to them."

Jesus Christ Heals the People and Blesses the Children
3 NEPHI 17

Jesus needed to visit other people besides the Nephites. He looked and saw the people watching Him with tears in their eyes. They wished Jesus would stay. So, Jesus decided to stay a little longer.

3 NEPHI 17

Jesus said, "Bring anyone who is sick, blind, or deaf. Bring anyone who cannot walk or speak or has any issue. If you bring them to me, I will heal them." So they brought their sick, and He healed them all.

3 NEPHI 17

Jesus asked them to bring their small children to Him. They sat the children on the ground all around Him. Jesus asked the adults to kneel down. Jesus knelt down too and prayed for the children.

3 NEPHI 17

Jesus said wonderful things in His prayer. They were so wonderful that they could not write them down. Jesus said, "You are blessed because of your faith. I am full of joy." Then He cried with happiness.

3 NEPHI 17

Jesus blessed each child one by one. He prayed for each child. He cried again with happiness. He told the parents, "Look at your children!"

3 NEPHI 17

When the parents looked, heaven opened up. Angels came down and circled around the children. It looked like they were surrounded by fire. The angels taught and helped the children.

Jesus Christ Teaches about the Sacrament
3 NEPHI 18

Jesus told the twelve disciples to get bread and wine. Jesus broke the bread in pieces and blessed it. He gave it to the disciples. They ate the bread. Then the disciples gave everyone else the bread to eat too.

101

3 NEPHI 18

Jesus taught, "Do this to remember my body, which I have shown to you. Eating this bread will show that you always remember me. If you always remember me, then you will have my Spirit to be with you."

3 NEPHI 18

Jesus took the wine and blessed it. He gave it to the disciples to drink. Then the disciples gave everyone else the wine to drink too. Jesus taught, "Drink this wine to remember my blood, which I shed for you.

3 NEPHI 18

Drinking this wine will show Heavenly Father you want to obey my commandments. I command everyone who is baptized to eat this bread and drink this wine. If you obey, you will be blessed."

3 NEPHI 18

Jesus continued to teach the people, "Pray always to protect yourself from Satan. He will always try to tempt you because he wants you to fail like he has. Pray for your families so they will be blessed.

3 NEPHI 18

God will give you every good thing you ask for. So meet and pray together in church often. Pray for each other, even those who aren't at church. Follow my example, and you will be a light to the world."

After Jesus said these things, He gave each of the twelve disciples the power to give the Gift of the Holy Ghost. Then a cloud came down and carried Jesus into heaven.

The Nephite Disciples Teach and Are Baptized
3 NEPHI 19

The people left and told their family and friends they had seen Jesus. They said He would come again. So many people traveled all night to Bountiful so they could see Jesus the next day.

3 NEPHI 19

Now the twelve disciples were Nephi; his brother Timothy, who Nephi raised from the dead; Nephi's son Jonas; Mathoni; Mathoni's brother, Mathonihah; Kumen; Kumenonhi; Jeremiah; Shemnon; Jonas; Zedekiah; and Isaiah.

3 NEPHI 19

The people gathered around the temple. The twelve disciples separated them into twelve groups. Each disciple took a group and taught them what Jesus had taught. They knelt down and prayed together.

3 NEPHI 19

Then everyone walked to the water. Nephi got in and was baptized first. Then Nephi baptized the other eleven disciples. Then they received the Holy Ghost. Heaven opened and angels came down.

3 NEPHI 19

The angels taught the twelve disciples. While they were teaching, Jesus came down from heaven and began to teach the disciples.

3 NEPHI 19

Jesus commanded that everyone kneel down and pray. While they prayed, Jesus walked a ways off and prayed to Heavenly Father. He prayed that everyone who believed would have the Holy Ghost.

3 NEPHI 19

Jesus stood up and returned to where the disciples were praying. Jesus smiled when he saw them. They were filled with light and were still praying.

Jesus Christ Prophesies of the Last Days
3 NEPHI 20–23, 29–30

Jesus commanded everyone to stand. He told them to continue praying in their hearts. Then Jesus made bread and wine appear. He blessed and passed it out as another sacrament for all the people.

3 NEPHI 20–23, 29–30

Jesus said they were part of His chosen people, called the House of Israel. In the last days, everyone will learn about God so He can gather all of His people together.

3 NEPHI 20–23, 29–30

Jesus told them that there will be a sign when this gathering begins. The sign will be when The Book of Mormon is translated and published.

3 NEPHI 20–23, 29–30

The Gentiles will also learn from The Book of Mormon. Everyone not part of the House of Israel is called a Gentile. If the Gentiles repent and obey God's words, they will join the House of Israel.

3 NEPHI 20–23, 29–30

In the last days, God's people will gather as part of one church. This church will be called Zion. Nothing will be able to destroy the church in the last days.

119

3 NEPHI 20–23, 29–30

Jesus told the people that the prophet Isaiah taught about the gathering of Israel. Jesus commanded His people to study Isaiah and all the prophets.

3 NEPHI 20–23, 29–30

Jesus told Nephi to go get his records. Jesus told Nephi to record one of Samuel the Lamanite's prophecies they had forgotten to write down.

3 NEPHI 20–23, 29–30

Samuel had said that when Jesus appeared, many saints would rise from the dead and teach the people. So Nephi wrote Samuel's prophecy down. He also wrote many other things Jesus taught.

The Prophet Malachi's Words
3 NEPHI 24–25

Jesus told the people to write down some of the prophet Malachi's words. Heavenly Father told Malachi that He would send Elijah the prophet before the Second Coming of Jesus Christ.

3 NEPHI 24–25

Malachi wrote, "Jesus Christ will be like the fire used to make silver. The fire burns very hot until the other metals and rock burn away. Only pure silver will be left. You are that silver.

3 NEPHI 24–25

Christ will judge you for not being true to your spouse. Or for lying. Or for not paying your employees enough. Or for not taking care of the widows and fatherless children. Or for sending foreigners away.

3 NEPHI 24–25

Also, many of you have stolen from God. You stole by not paying your tithing. If you pay tithing, God will give you more blessings than you can handle.

3 NEPHI 24–25

Jesus keeps a book of names. If you do and say good things, your name gets written down. That is how we will know who serves Christ and who does not.

3 NEPHI 24–25

In the final days, those who don't follow Jesus Christ will suffer. Those who do follow Jesus Christ will be protected and healed by Him. You will know the final days are near when Elijah restores baptisms for the dead."

3 NEPHI 24–25

When Jesus was done telling them the prophet Malachi's words, He said, "God told me you did not have these scriptures. So, God commanded me to give them to you. You can now teach them to your children."

129

The Disciples Continue To Teach and Baptize
3 NEPHI 26

The prophet Mormon wrote that there were many more things Jesus taught the people. Mormon was going to write more, but God told him not to. God wants to test our faith with the scriptures we have.

3 NEPHI 26

At the day of judgment, every single person will take turns in front of God. God will judge every one of us. If we were good, then we will live forever with God. If we weren't, we won't get to live with God.

3 NEPHI 26

When Jesus Christ showed Himself, He taught the people for three days. He also taught and blessed the children. Babies and children taught their parents many wonderful things that cannot be written down.

3 NEPHI 26

Once Jesus left, the disciples began to travel. They taught and baptized as many people as they could. Everyone became members of the church.

Jesus Christ Appears Again to the Nephite Disciples
3 NEPHI 27–28

One day, the disciples were praying and fasting together. While they were praying, Jesus showed Himself to them. Jesus told them to name the church, The Church of Jesus Christ.

3 NEPHI 27–28

Jesus also taught them the gospel, "Repent and be baptized in my name. Then you will receive the Holy Ghost. The Holy Ghost will make your spirits clean. Continue to obey, and you will be saved.

135

3 NEPHI 27–28

Follow my example. Do the things you have seen me do. If you do, then you will be saved. Remember this: you will be given anything you ask Heavenly Father for if it is good and you ask in my name.

3 NEPHI 27–28

Now write these things down. The people will be judged whether or not they follow what you write down. Everyone will be judged by the words written in the scriptures.

3 NEPHI 27–28

I am full of joy because of you and all the people choosing good. Heavenly Father and all the angels too are full of joy because of you."

3 NEPHI 27–28

Then Jesus asked, "What do you desire most from me after I return to Heavenly Father?" Nine of the disciples asked if they could return to live with Heavenly Father and Jesus in heaven after they died.

3 NEPHI 27–28

Jesus said, "You are blessed because you want this good thing. I bless you that when you die, you will return to my kingdom." Then Jesus asked the other three disciples what they wanted.

3 NEPHI 27–28

The three disciples weren't sure they should ask for what they wanted. They said nothing. Jesus said to them, "Don't be sorry for what you wish. I know your thoughts and what you want.

141

3 NEPHI 27–28

You wish to stay on earth and never die, so you can keep helping people repent. I bless you to never die. You will remain until I return again. You three are more blessed for wanting this."

3 NEPHI 27–28

When Jesus finished speaking, He touched the nine disciples with his finger. Then He left. The twelve received wonderful visions from heaven. They continued preaching to the people and baptizing them.

3 NEPHI 27–28

Not everyone believed the disciples. Some put the disciples into prison, but the prisons broke. Some threw them into fire, but they didn't get burned. Some put them with wild animals, but they didn't get hurt.

3 NEPHI 27–28

Anyone who believed the disciples was baptized. They became members of The Church of Jesus Christ. The disciples continued to preach the gospel of Jesus Christ.

Three Hundred Years of Nephite Righteousness
4 NEPHI

Three years had passed since Jesus Christ appeared in Bountiful. The twelve disciples preached and baptized until everyone believed and was baptized.

4 NEPHI

Everyone cared for each other. They shared all their things. There were no poor or rich. There were no prisoners or robbers. Everyone treated each other kindly and honestly.

4 NEPHI

There was peace throughout the land. The disciples continued to work miracles. They healed the sick, helped the blind to see and the deaf to hear, and raised the dead. They did all this in Jesus Christ's name.

4 NEPHI

The people rebuilt their cities. They got married and had children. They grew to be a great people. Everyone followed the gospel of Jesus Christ. They went to church, they prayed, and they fasted.

4 NEPHI

The people lived happily like this for two hundred years. Then the people began to care more about their belongings than the church. The people became more and more wicked.

4 NEPHI

After another one hundred years, almost everyone in the land was wicked. The prophet Nephi had kept the records before giving them to his son Amos.

4 NEPHI

Amos kept the records before giving them to his son, also called Amos. His son Amos kept the records until he died. Then his brother Ammaron kept the records.

4 NEPHI

Ammaron kept the records for a while. Soon the Holy Ghost told Ammaron to hide the sacred records. So Ammaron took the records and buried them in a hill.

Mormon

Mormon Is Visited by Jesus Christ
MORMON 1

Ammaron met a ten-year-old boy named Mormon. "You are a calm, thoughtful, and obedient child. When you are older, go to the hill Shim. You will find the Nephite records. Write what happens to our people."

MORMON 1

Mormon lived in Zarahemla. In his day, the people were very wicked. But Mormon was good and steady. When he was fifteen, Jesus Christ visited him. Mormon experienced the goodness of Jesus.

Mormon tried to teach the people to repent. But the Holy Ghost made him stop. The people already knew what they were supposed to do. The people chose not to obey God and His commandments on purpose.

Mormon Commands the Nephite Army
MORMON 2

Mormon was a large, strong boy. When he turned sixteen, the Nephites decided to make him the leader of all their armies. The Lamanites came to battle.

MORMON 2

Mormon led the Nephite armies to fight, but they got scared. The Nephite army began to run away instead. The Lamanites chased them from the city of Angola to the land of Joshua.

161

The Nephites gathered in Joshua. The Lamanite king, Aaron, came and destroyed many of the Nephites. The land was also filled with robbers who stole many things. But the Nephites would not repent.

MORMON 2

The Nephites felt sad because they couldn't sin and be happy at the same time. They were angry with God. Mormon became sad because they chose not to repent.

MORMON 2

The Nephites ran away again to a city called Jashon. This city was near the hill where Ammaron hid the records. Mormon went and got the plates of Nephi and began to write everything happening to his people.

MORMON 2

Again, the Nephites had to escape to a different city, which was called Shem. Here the Nephites began to beat the Lamanites in battle. Finally, the Nephites and Lamanites decided to stop fighting each other.

Mormon Preaches to the Nephites
MORMON 3

The Nephites took the land in the north. The Lamanites took the land in the south. Mormon made the Nephites prepare themselves. He knew the Lamanites would come back to fight again.

MORMON 3

God told Mormon to tell the Nephites to repent. Mormon tried, but the Nephites would not listen. They had stopped caring about God.

MORMON 3

After ten years of no fighting, the Lamanites came to battle again. The Nephites took their armies to the city called Desolation to defend themselves. Mormon helped the Nephites win.

MORMON 3

The Nephites believed their strength helped them win—not God's help. The Nephites wanted to attack the Lamanites this time. Mormon refused. He chose not to lead the Nephite armies anymore.

MORMON 3

The Nephites would pay for their own sins because they chose not to repent. Everyone must be judged for the good or bad they have done.

Mormon Gathers the Nephite Records
MORMON 4

The Nephites and Lamanites battled each other again and again. Sometimes the Nephites won. Sometimes the Lamanites won.

MORMON 4

The Nephites and Lamanites were the most wicked of all God's children. Mormon learned that one way God punishes the wicked is by letting them hurt each other.

MORMON 4

They battled for many years. Finally, the Nephites began to lose. Mormon saw that the Lamanites would soon win. So Mormon gathered up all the records Ammaron hid in the hill Shim.

The Book of Mormon Testifies of Jesus Christ
MORMON 5

The Nephites were about to all be destroyed. So Mormon decided to return and help them. But Mormon knew they would still die even with his help. They would die because they would not repent.

MORMON 5

Mormon wrote that the stories in The Book of Mormon were to help us believe in Jesus Christ. They help us understand that Jesus Christ is Heavenly Father's Son. They help us learn the gospel of Jesus Christ.

When we stop believing in Jesus Christ, Satan has power over us. When we stop obeying the gospel, we are like a boat without a steering wheel and sail. We get tossed by the waves, unable to go anywhere.

Believe in Jesus Christ. Obey His gospel. Repent of your sins. Be humble. This means don't think you know better than God; trust in Him enough to obey Him. He will remember the prayers of those who obey.

The Battle at Cumorah
MORMON 6

Mormon wrote a letter to the king of the Lamanites. He asked the king to let the Nephites gather all the rest of their people. They would fight the Lamanites by the Hill Cumorah after the Nephites gathered.

MORMON 6

Mormon was now an old man. He knew the Nephites would die soon. He took all the records and buried them in the Hill Cumorah. Mormon gave the last set of plates to his son Moroni.

MORMON 6

The Nephites and Lamanites had one last battle. Over two hundred thousand Nephites died. Only Moroni and twenty-four other Nephites were still alive. Mormon was alive too, but he was wounded.

Mormon's Testimony
MORMON 7

Mormon gave his final testimony: "My people, you must no longer fight. Believe in Jesus Christ, repent of your sins, and be baptized.

MORMON 7

Christ died and came back to life, so we can too. Our spirits and bodies will come back together. We will stand in front of God. He will judge us for all the good and bad we did. Follow the gospel of Jesus Christ.

MORMON 7

Repent, be baptized, and receive the Holy Ghost. If you obey this gospel, you can enter God's kingdom. To have the Holy Ghost be with you, you must obey and live God's commandments."

Moroni Gets the Plates
MORMON 8

Moroni wrote on the plates. He said after the great battle on the Hill Cumorah, the Lamanites found and killed Mormon.

MORMON 8

Moroni was now the last Nephite alive. The land was filled with Lamanites and robbers. They fought with each other.

MORMON 8

Moroni would finish writing on the plates and bury them. He said one day God would let the plates be found. The words written on the plates would be shared with the whole earth.

MORMON 8

The world will be a wicked place when the plates are found. People will no longer believe in or follow God. They will build churches to make money for themselves.

Moroni Writes to Us in the Latter Days
MORMON 9

Moroni wrote to us who live in the latter days. He said, "I speak to those who do not believe in Jesus Christ. Pray to God in Jesus Christ's name.

If you do not believe in miracles or revelations, then you don't understand the scriptures. The scriptures teach that God does not change. He will always be a God of miracles and revelation.

MORMON 9

God created the heavens and the earth. God created Adam and Eve. Because of them, all people on earth are alive. Because of them, they can also sin. So God sent Jesus Christ to save us all from sin.

Because of Jesus Christ we can all live again after we die. When we are resurrected, we will return to God. God will judge us. If we are good and clean, we will be happy."

Ether

God Doesn't Change the Jaredite Language
ETHER 1

King Limhi's people had found the Jaredite records on twenty-four plates. The Jaredite records told the stories of the creation and Adam and Eve. It had many stories written up through the Tower of Babel.

ETHER 1

The Jaredite record was written by the prophet Ether. Ether was a descendant of Jared. Jared lived at the time the people built the Tower of Babel, when God changed everyone's language.

The brother of Jared was called Mahonri Moriancumer. Mahonri was a large and mighty man. God loved Mahonri very much. Jared asked Mahonri to pray to God: "Ask Him to not change our language."

ETHER 1

Mahonri prayed that God would not change the language of his family or friends. God heard his prayer and didn't change their language. Mahonri also asked if they should leave and go somewhere else.

ETHER 1

God told Mahonri to gather his family and their friends. God commanded them to pack their things and move to a valley north of the city. From there, God would lead them to a promised land.

The Jaredites Travel and Build Boats
ETHER 2

Mahonri and Jared's people gathered things for their journey. They brought all their animals. They even brought fish, bees, and seeds. Then they went up to the valley Nimrod that God had revealed to them.

When they arrived, God came down in a cloud and spoke with Mahonri, the brother of Jared. Mahonri couldn't see God, but he could hear Him. God commanded Mahonri to lead the people into the desert.

ETHER 2

So the families obeyed. God continued to help them while they traveled. God directed them where to go. He would continue leading them to the promised land.

ETHER 2

God told Mahonri that He had blessed the promised land. If the people obeyed God, then they would be blessed. If they didn't obey God, they would be destroyed.

After many days, the people called the Jaredites arrived at the ocean. They pitched their tents. They called the seashore Moriancumer. They stayed for four years before God spoke with Mahonri again.

God was not happy with Mahonri, the brother of Jared, because he had forgotten to pray. Mahonri repented. God forgave him. God warned him to keep praying, or else the Spirit could not guide him.

God showed Mahonri how to build special boats. God commanded the Jaredites to build them. The boats were small, lightweight, and tight like a dish. They were closed so tight that air and light could not get into the boat.

When the Jaredites finished, Mahonri prayed to God. "God, we have finished building eight boats like you have shown us. But they are so tight that we cannot see or breathe in them. We will die in them."

ETHER 2

God told Mahonri, the brother of Jared, to cut a small hole in the top and bottom of each boat. If the Jaredites needed air, they could pull out a plug to breathe. Mahonri obeyed and cut holes in the boats.

Mahonri prayed again, "God, we obeyed and cut holes in the boats. But there is still no light in them. Do you wish us to travel in the dark?" God answered, "What should I do so that you have light in the boats?

Windows will break, and you can't have fire in the boats. These boats will travel like whales under the water. Waves and wind will push you toward the promised land. So tell me what you would like me to do."

Mahonri Sees Jesus Christ
ETHER 3

Mahonri, the brother of Jared, went up the mountain Shelem. There he melted a rock into sixteen small stones. The stones were clear as glass. He took them to the top of the mountain and prayed to God.

ETHER 3

God, You gave us a commandment to pray to You if we need something. Please don't let us travel in darkness. I know if You touch these small stones, they will shine light in the boats."

ETHER 3

Jesus Christ reached down and touched each stone with His finger to make them shine. Mahonri saw Jesus's finger. He fell onto the ground afraid. Jesus said, "Stand. Why did you fall?"

ETHER 3

"I saw Your finger. I didn't know You had a body of flesh and blood," said Mahonri. "Because of your faith, you were able to see me. Did you see more than my finger?" Jesus replied. "No," said Mahonri. "Show Yourself to me."

ETHER 3

"Will you believe my words?" asked Jesus. "I know You will only tell the truth," said Mahonri. So Jesus showed Himself to Mahonri. "You are saved. Because of your great faith, you can see me," said Jesus.

ETHER 3

"I am Jesus Christ. I will save whoever believes in me. No one has believed in me as much as you have. Do you see how your body was made like my body? This is my spirit body now. Later, I will have a body of flesh.

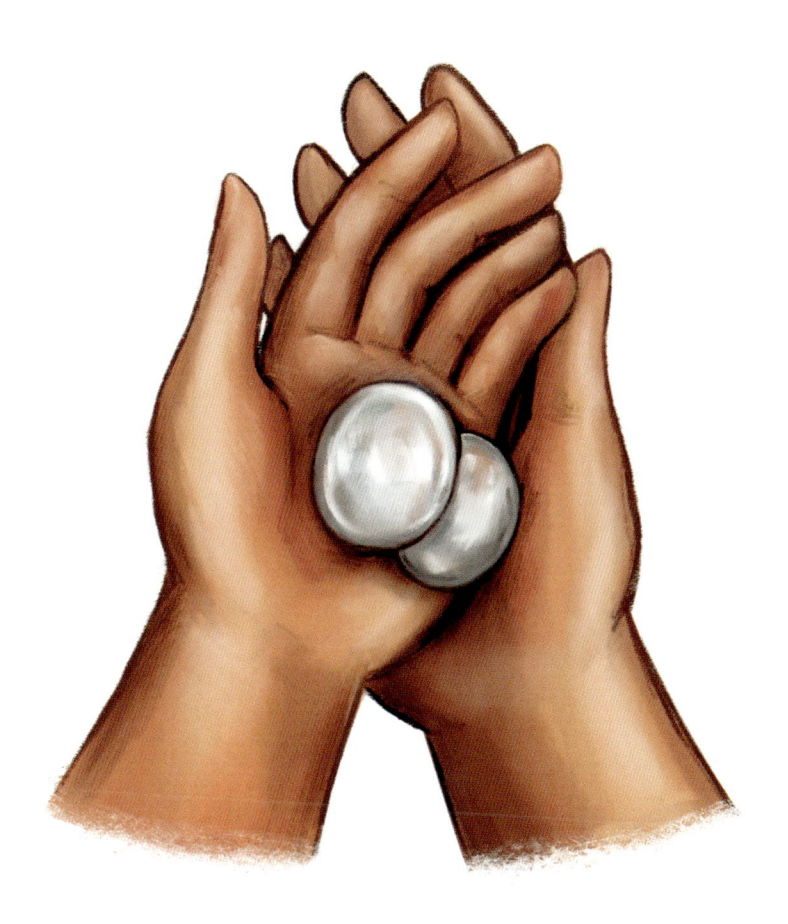

Now, Mahonri, do not tell anyone what you saw and heard today. Just write it down." He then gave two stones to Mahonri and said, "One day, I will let others read your record using these two stones."

ETHER 3

Then Jesus showed Mahonri the history of the earth, from the beginning to the end. "Write down everything I have shown you. Hide the record and the stones together. One day, everyone will read your record."

Moroni Adds the Jaredite Records to the Gold Plates
ETHER 4–5

Moroni took what Mahonri, the brother of Jared, had written and copied it to the Gold Plates. God commanded Moroni to seal and hide them with the two stone interpreters Jesus gave Mahonri.

ETHER 4–5

Mahonri's records won't be shared until the non-believers repent and have faith. Then Jesus Christ will explain His revelations. Moroni wrote that those who don't believe won't be shown anything else.

ETHER 4–5

Those who believe will receive the Spirit and know that the records are true. They will know the records are true because they teach us to do good. Anything that leads you to do good comes from Jesus Christ.

ETHER 4–5

Jesus said, "Come to me, and I will give you knowledge. Repent, believe my gospel, and be baptized. Then you will be saved. Whoever follows my commandments until the end will live with me in heaven."

ETHER 4–5

Moroni explained that the Gold Plates would be shown to three witnesses. These three witnesses would share their testimony that The Book of Mormon is true.

The Jaredites Multiply and Choose a King
ETHER 6

Mahonri took the two stone interpreters and the sixteen stones that Jesus touched. He walked back down the mountain. He put two stones in each boat for light while they traveled across the ocean.

ETHER 6

The people prepared food, water, and their animals. They got into the boats and set off. God created a great wind that began to push the boats. The wind never stopped blowing them toward the promised land.

225

ETHER 6

The boats often went under the water, but they didn't leak. Whales couldn't harm them. Mahonri and his people praised God. They traveled for three hundred forty-four days before arriving at the promised land.

ETHER 6

They landed on shore and thanked God for blessing them. The Jaredites began to build and farm on the land. Altogether, there were twenty-two Jaredites who traveled across the ocean.

ETHER 6

Soon the Jaredites began to have many children. They were all taught to follow God and His commandments. They grew to become a strong and humble people.

ETHER 6

When Mahonri and Jared grew old, they gathered their families. They asked their families if they wanted anything before they died. They asked for Mahonri and Jared to choose someone to be their king.

ETHER 6

This made Mahonri and Jared worried. They knew kings weren't always good. But they let the people choose a king. Each of Mahonri and Jared's sons refused to be king except for Jared's son Orihah.

ETHER 6

Orihah became their king. He was a good and humble king who taught his people to follow God. The people soon grew very rich. After some time, Jared and Mahonri grew old and died.

The Jaredites Begin To Fight Each Other
ETHER 7

Orihah lived a long time and had many children. He had thirty-one children. One of his sons was named Kib. Orihah made Kib the king. Kib had many children too. One of Kib's sons was called Corihor.

Corihor was not a good person. He didn't like obeying his father. He ran away to a place called Nehor. While in Nehor, Corihor had many children. His daughters were beautiful, and his sons were handsome.

ETHER 7

Corihor's children got others to leave Kib's kingdom. When enough people had left the kingdom, Corihor led them back and took over the city. He put his father, Kib, in prison.

ETHER 7

While Kib was in prison, he had another son named Shule. Shule grew up to be a very strong and wise man. Now Shule was angry with Corihor for what he did to their father, Kib.

ETHER 7

Shule and others escaped from Corihor. Shule went to a hill called Ephraim and made swords for everyone who had escaped. They took their swords and went back to the city to fight Corihor.

236

ETHER 7

Shule freed his father, Kib, from prison. Kib made Shule king over the people. Corihor felt very sorry for everything he had done. Shule saw his brother was sorry, so he let Corihor help him rule the kingdom.

ETHER 7

One of Corihor's sons was named Noah. Noah was angry with his uncle Shule and his father, Corihor. So Noah got his brother and many of the people to fight against Shule.

ETHER 7

Noah and his army took over part of the land. The people who followed Noah made him their king in that part of the land. Noah also captured Shule and put him in prison.

ETHER 7

Noah planned to kill Shule. Before he could, Shule's sons snuck into Noah's house and killed him first. Shule's sons broke down the prison door and helped their father escape.

Noah's son Cohor became king. Cohor fought against Shule but was killed in battle. Nimrod, Cohor's son, gave the kingdom back to Shule. Shule was so thankful that he gave Nimrod many gifts.

ETHER 7

While Shule was king, the people began to disobey God's commandments. So God called prophets to help the people repent. The prophets told the Jaredites they would be destroyed if they did not repent.

Many of the Jaredites made fun of the prophets. They argued with the prophets. When King Shule saw this, he made a law. The law let the prophets teach wherever they wanted to in his kingdom.

ETHER 7

Because of Shule's law and the prophets' teachings, the people finally repented. Because the people repented, God did not destroy them. Again the Jaredites were blessed and began to be very rich.

ETHER 7

Shule began to be old. He was a good king who followed God's commandments. He always reminded himself of God's goodness for leading the Jaredites across the ocean.

Akish and the Secret Society
ETHER 8

Shule had a son named Omer who became king. Omer's son Jared was disobedient. Jared decided to leave the kingdom to go to a place called Heth. There he began to build an army.

ETHER 8

Once Jared had an army, he took over the kingdom and locked his father in prison. Jared's brothers Esrom and Coriantumr fought back and beat him. When Jared lost the kingdom, it made him very sad.

ETHER 8

Jared's daughter was very beautiful and smart. She didn't like seeing her father so sad. She made a plan. She told her father to invite over a man named Akish. When Akish came, Jared's daughter danced for him.

ETHER 8

Akish asked Jared if he could marry his daughter. Jared said, "I will let you marry her, if you kill my father, King Omer." Omer and Akish were friends, but Akish agreed to Jared's plan because he wanted power.

ETHER 8

Akish called his family and friends together. They promised to help Akish and to keep it a secret. They created a secret society—a secret group that does evil things. These secret groups come from Satan.

ETHER 8

Moroni warned us to be careful of these secret societies. Any country with secret societies will be destroyed. Secret societies don't care about anyone's freedom. They only want power and money.

The Jaredites Nearly Destroy Themselves
ETHER 9

Akish and his secret society made plans to kill King Omer. But God warned Omer in a dream. So Omer took his family and left the city. They traveled far away to a place by the sea called Ablom.

Jared became king, and he gave Akish his daughter to marry for helping him. But Akish wanted to be king. So Akish got his secret society together. They killed Jared and made Akish king.

ETHER 9

One of Akish's sons did not like what his father was doing. He took some of his friends and they left to live with Omer and his family. Akish's other sons were like Akish. They only cared about power and money.

Soon, Akish and his sons began to battle each other. Everyone in the city either fought for Akish or one of his sons. They fought for many years. Finally, everyone in the city was destroyed, except for thirty people.

Omer and his family returned. Omer was very old, so he made his son Emer the king. King Emer was a good king who followed God. Emer's people grew wealthy and had peace for sixty-two years.

ETHER 9

Emer made his son Coriantum king. Coriantum was a good king. And Coriantum's son Com was also a good king. But Com's son Heth was not a good man. Heth had his secret society make him king.

ETHER 9

God saw that the Jaredites were beginning to be wicked. So God sent prophets to tell the people to repent or be destroyed. The people did not listen. They threw the prophets out of their cities.

ETHER 9

The Jaredites would not repent, so God did not let it rain. Without rain, no food could grow. God also sent snakes to scare their animals away. The Jaredites began to starve without anything to eat or drink.

259

ETHER 9

Once the Jaredites saw they were about to die, they began to repent. They prayed for forgiveness. When they had repented enough, God sent them rain. And food began to grow again.

Wicked Kings Lead to Destruction
ETHER 10–11

Heth's son Shez began to rebuild the kingdom and his people. Shez was a good king who followed God's commandments. When Shez grew old, he gave the kingdom to his son Riplakish.

261

ETHER 10–11

Riplakish did not follow God's commandments. Riplakish decided to marry many women. He also taxed the people a lot. He used the tax money to build large, beautiful buildings.

ETHER 10–11

If the people couldn't pay their taxes, he put them into prison. In prison, he forced the people to make nice things for his buildings. After many years, the people killed Riplakish and forced his family to run away.

ETHER 10–11

Riplakish's son Morianton gathered an army and took back the kingdom. He lowered their taxes and was a good king to the people. But Morianton did not obey God's commandments in his own life.

The Jaredites had many kings. Some kings were good and followed God's commandments. Other kings were not good and caused the people to sin. The Jaredites worked hard, so they had many nice things.

ETHER 10–11

Whenever the people began to be wicked, God would send prophets. The prophets would warn the people to repent or be destroyed. Sometimes the people listened and were saved. Other times the people did not listen, so many of them were destroyed.

Faith, Hope, and Grace
ETHER 12

After many years, there was a king named Coriantumr. God sent a prophet to Coriantumr and his people. This prophet was called Ether.

ETHER 12

Ether was a great prophet. He tried to warn the people they would be destroyed if they did not believe in God and repent. Ether warned the people from sunrise to sunset.

ETHER 12

Ether taught the people many great and wonderful things, but the people did not believe him. They didn't believe because they couldn't see Ether's prophecies.

ETHER 12

Moroni explained that trusting and believing in something you cannot see yet is called faith. Faith leads us to act even though we cannot see what will happen next.

ETHER 12

If we have faith in Jesus Christ, it means we believe in Him enough to do the things He has taught, even if we don't know why. God can do many things for us if we just have faith.

ETHER 12

There have been many things that were done through faith. Mahonri, the brother of Jared, believed in Jesus Christ so much that he saw Christ's finger touch the stones.

ETHER 12

Because of Alma and Amulek's faith, they broke free of the ropes they were tied with. Because of their faith, the prison they were in crumbled to the earth, and they were not hurt.

ETHER 12

Because of Nephi and Lehi's faith, thousands of Lamanites repented and were baptized. Because of their faith, a pillar of fire surrounded them in prison to show God's power to the Lamanites.

ETHER 12

Because of Ammon and his brothers' faith, many Lamanites came to know the truth. Because of their faith, they had the spirit of prophecy and revelation. They had been given great power and authority from God.

ETHER 12

The three Nephite disciples showed faith too. Because of their faith, they received a promise that they would never die. Miracles only happen when someone first believes in God and acts in faith.

ETHER 12

Mahonri's faith was so strong, he said, "Move!" to a mountain, and it moved! Faith is important, but we must also be humble. Being humble means you trust God more than you trust anyone else, including yourself.

ETHER 12

When we are humble, we care more about what God cares about. We care less about what the world cares about. We don't think we are better than other people.

ETHER 12

If we are humble and choose to do whatever God wants, then God will show us our weakness. God gives everyone weakness so we may learn to trust Him.

ETHER 12

If we are humble and have faith in Jesus Christ, then He will give us strength, called grace. He will help us do good things we could not do without His help.

The Prophet Ether Warns King Coriantumr
ETHER 13

Ether taught the Jaredites about many great and important things. But the people did not believe him. They threw him out of the city.

ETHER 13

Ether had to hide in a cave. At night, Ether would come out of the cave and watch what happened to the people. He would write down everything he saw happening.

ETHER 13

Ether watched as a great war broke out among Coriantumr's people. There were many strong men who tried to take the kingdom away from Coriantumr. But Coriantumr was strong and fought against them.

ETHER 13

God told Ether to go give Coriantumr a message. Ether obeyed. He told Coriantumr that if he and his family repented, God would let Coriantumr keep his kingdom. God would also save all the Jaredites.

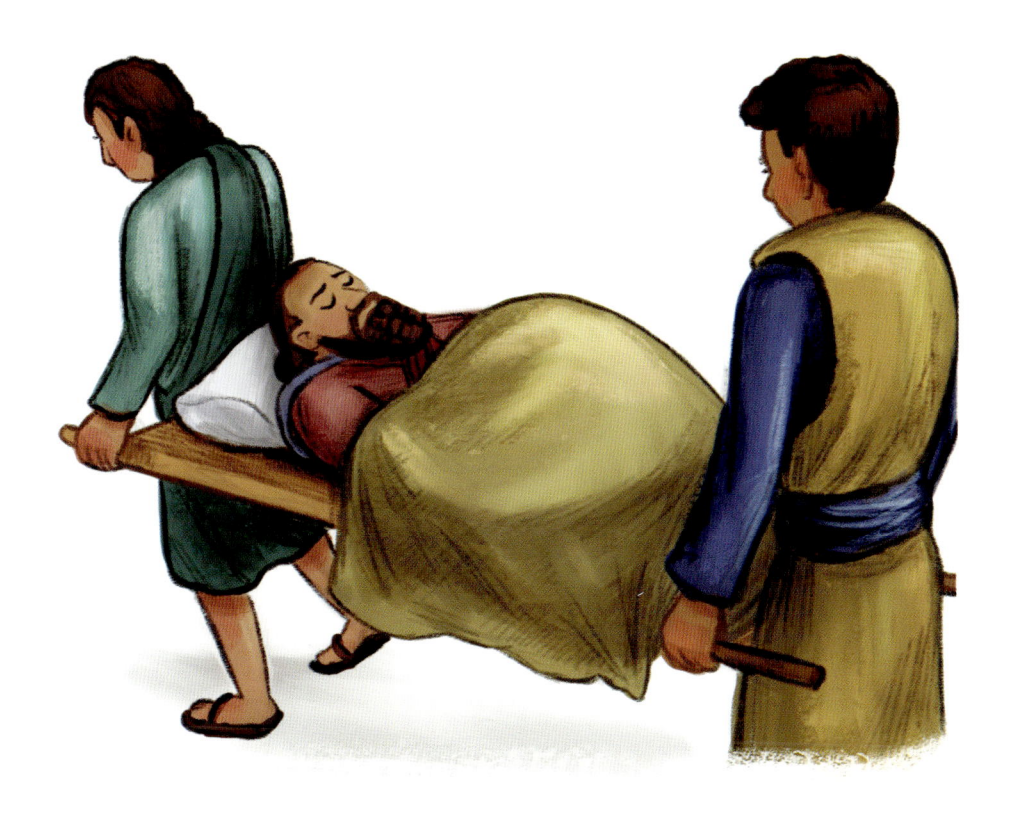

If Coriantumr and his family did not repent, all the Jaredites would be destroyed. God would let Coriantumr live long enough to watch everyone die. He would see the Nephites take over the land. Then he would die.

ETHER 13

Coriantumr and his family did not repent. They tried to kill Ether. Ether ran away and hid in his cave. Coriantumr continued his war against everyone who tried to take his kingdom away.

ETHER 13

Now there was another man named Shared who fought against Coriantumr. They battled against each other many times until Coriantumr finally beat and killed Shared.

Coriantumr Fights Gilead, Lib, Then Shiz
ETHER 14

A curse fell over the land. If the people didn't hold onto their things, their things would disappear. They always had to carry their swords with them to defend themselves.

ETHER 14

Shared's brother Gilead was angry with Coriantumr. Gilead fought Coriantumr. Gilead attacked Coriantumr's men at night while they were drunk. He won and took over the kingdom.

ETHER 14

For two years, Coriantumr stayed in the wilderness and built up his army. Gilead continued to rule the kingdom. But there was a secret society that killed Gilead and made another man king. His name was Lib.

ETHER 14

Coriantumr battled King Lib. When Lib died, his brother became king. His name was Shiz. Shiz was a very strong man who fought very hard. He fought Coriantumr and chased his people for many days.

ETHER 14

Shiz and Coriantumr's armies fought against each other for many days. One day, while they were fighting, Shiz wounded Coriantumr so badly that Coriantumr fainted. Everyone thought he was dead.

The Jaredites Completely Destroy Themselves
ETHER 15

Coriantumr was not dead. He healed from his wounds. While he was healing, he remembered Ether's words. Coriantumr would live long enough to watch all his people die. Two million people had already died.

Coriantumr began to repent. He wanted his people to live. So Coriantumr wrote a letter to Shiz asking him for peace. But Shiz and his people were angry with Coriantumr. Instead, they came to battle him again.

ETHER 15

So Coriantumr and his army battled Shiz and his army. They battled again and again. Ether watched as all the Jaredites fought each other. Everyone fought for either Shiz or Coriantumr.

ETHER 15

The Jaredites gathered for battle near the Hill Cumorah. Both armies made every man, woman, and child wear armor and fight in the battle. They fought all day long, but no one won.

ETHER 15

Coriantumr sent another letter to Shiz asking for peace, but Shiz refused. So both armies fought day after day. Finally, Shiz only had thirty-two people left. Coriantumr only had twenty-seven people left.

ETHER 15

On the last day of fighting, everyone died except for Coriantumr and Shiz. Shiz was wounded and fainted. Coriantumr rested for a while on his sword. Then Coriantumr killed Shiz and fainted too.

ETHER 15

Ether finished his record. He took his records and hid them where they could be found by the Nephites. Ether's final words said, "It doesn't matter what happens to me now, as long as I am saved in God's kingdom. Amen."

Moroni

Laying on of Hands, Ordaining, and the Sacrament
MORONI 1–5

Moroni hid from the Lamanites. He wrote a few more things down on the plates. He wanted to share more about what Jesus said and did when He came and visited the Nephites.

MORONI 1–5

Jesus Christ told His twelve Nephite disciples to pray to God in Christ's name. They had the power to give the gift of the Holy Ghost to others. The disciples did this by laying their hands on the person's head.

MORONI 1–5

The disciples ordained priests and teachers. Ordain means to bless someone and invite them to help God. The priests and teachers taught the people to have faith in Jesus Christ and repent of their sins.

MORONI 1–5

Jesus showed the disciples how to bless the sacrament. The sacrament helps us remember Jesus Christ's Atonement. When we take the sacrament, we promise to remember Jesus Christ and keep His commandments.

Being Members of The Church of Jesus Christ
MORONI 6

Jesus Christ taught about baptism. We're ready for baptism when we feel sorry for things we have done wrong, trust God enough to obey His commandments, and have changed how we think and act.

MORONI 6

When we are baptized, we promise to be an example of Jesus Christ, the power of the Holy Ghost cleans away our sins, and we become a member of The Church of Jesus Christ.

The members of the church write down our names when we're baptized, so we don't forget each other. We help each other. We teach each other the words of God. We pray together and follow Jesus Christ.

MORONI 6

As members of the church, we meet together often to fast and to pray. We teach each other how to return to God. We meet to have the sacrament and show we remember Jesus Christ and our promises to Him.

MORONI 6

In all of our meetings, we follow the Spirit. The power of the Holy Ghost will help us know when to teach, pray, ask for forgiveness, repent, or sing.

Mormon Teaches about Faith, Hope, and Charity
MORONI 7

Moroni shared one of his father's talks from church. Mormon said in his talk, "Watch what people do. If they do good things, then they are also good people.

MORONI 7

All good things come from God. Everything else comes from Satan. God gave us the Spirit to help us know when something is good or not. If you choose to do good things, then you will have the Spirit.

MORONI 7

Angels and prophets have said Jesus Christ will come. Believe in Jesus and trust Him—this is called faith. Believe God will answer your prayers. If you pray to God in Jesus Christ's name with faith, He will answer you.

MORONI 7

God's angels show themselves to anyone who has strong faith. Angels always teach of Jesus Christ. They teach us to repent and keep our promises with God. These promises are called covenants.

MORONI 7

Jesus tells us to repent and be baptized. If we do, we can be saved. Being saved is called salvation. Salvation means we get to live with God again in heaven.

When we have hope, we are sure God will keep His promises to us. We can hope for salvation because of Jesus Christ's Atonement and resurrection. Jesus Christ's experience suffering in the Garden of Gethsemane and on the cross is called the Atonement.

MORONI 7

Having faith and hope in Jesus Christ will make us happy, calm, and courageous. We must also love others the way God does. This kind of love is called charity. You know you have charity when you are calm and kind to others.

MORONI 7

You have charity when you care about everyone, even people who are hard to love. This is how Jesus Christ loves everyone. If we try to love like Him, we cannot fail. We are nothing if we don't try to love as He does. So pray to God that you will always have this love."

Mormon Teaches about Baptism
MORONI 8

Mormon wrote Moroni a letter when Moroni started serving in the church. Mormon wrote the letter because the Nephites Moroni was teaching wanted to baptize their little children.

MORONI 8

Mormon wrote, "I prayed to God to know the truth. God sent the Holy Ghost who told me little children cannot sin. Only people who can sin need to repent and be baptized. Little children are saved by Jesus Christ.

MORONI 8

Those who don't know God's laws are also saved by Jesus. You have to know you broke God's law before you can repent. So they are not guilty. The first sign that you have repented is baptism.

MORONI 8

When you have faith in Jesus Christ, you will want to be baptized. After baptism, God forgives your sins when you obey His commandments. When God forgives you, you will feel calm and confident. The Holy Ghost will fill you with hope and charity."

The Nephites and Lamanites Are Wicked
MORONI 9

In another letter, Mormon wrote, "I am worried the Lamanites will destroy the Nephites. The Nephites don't repent. They are always angry with each other. I am still trying to teach them to choose the right.

MORONI 9

When I teach them what God has said, the Nephites either get angry with me or they don't listen. I worry the Spirit can no longer help them. They don't care about anything anymore, not even their own lives.

MORONI 9

Even though they won't listen, Moroni, we must still teach them. God commanded us to teach while we are still alive. If we do, we will live with God in His kingdom again.

MORONI 9

The Lamanites have taken many men, women, and children as prisoners. They kill the men. So the widows, daughters, and old women are left to suffer. But the Nephites do even worse things to the Lamanites!

MORONI 9

Moroni, I know I will see you soon. I have the Gold Plates that I need to give to you. Have faith in Jesus Christ. Have hope that we will someday live forever in heaven with God. Amen."

Moroni's Final Testimony
MORONI 10

"I, Moroni, ask that when you read The Book of Mormon, remember how kind and patient God has been to all His children. Think about His kindness, and feel it in your heart. Pray when you get the scriptures.

MORONI 10

Ask God in Jesus Christ's name if the scriptures are not true. Make sure you want to know the truth. Be willing to change your life if they are true. Believe in Jesus Christ. Then God will tell you the record is true with the Holy Ghost.

MORONI 10

The Holy Ghost has power. His power can help us know all true things. All good things are true. All good things show that Jesus Christ lives. The power of the Holy Ghost will help you know that Jesus Christ is real.

MORONI 10

God gives us special gifts through the Spirit to help us. Some have the gift of faith or the gift of healing or the gift of teaching. There are many gifts God can give us. He will always give us gifts, unless we stop believing in Him.

MORONI 10

Come to Christ. If you are good and love God, He will help you become perfect. As God helps you become perfect, you will be blessed and cleansed from sin. I will meet you after this life when Jesus Christ comes to judge us all. Amen.

About the Author and Illustrator

Author

Jason Zippro holds a master's degree in education from the University of Missouri-Saint Louis, a master's degree in business administration from the University of Utah, and a bachelor of arts degree in Italian with a minor in editing from Brigham Young University. Jason worked as an editor for four years before teaching 8th grade English for three years in Kansas City with the non-profit Teach for America. Jason and his wife, Sharolee, have four young children.

Illustrator

Alycia Pace graduated from Brigham Young University with a bachelor of fine arts degree in animation and is a freelance illustrator from her home in Utah. She has written and illustrated several books including *Polly the Perfectly Polite Pig* (available at Deseret Book and Barnes & Noble) and soon to be available, *How to Train a Dinosaur to Use the Potty*. She loves the smell of bookstores and exploring new places with her two children and adventurous husband.